Unlocking the Greatness Within
10 Steps to Empower Young People to Find Their Personal Greatness

by Abiodun Rashaun Banjo

Please note that I don't make any guarantees regarding the results of the information applied in this book. The resources shared are intended to help you succeed as a mentor, coach, teacher, parent, and/or overall youth leader. Nevertheless, outcomes will be the result of your own efforts, your particular situation, and innumerable other circumstances beyond my knowledge and control.

prolificconsultingservices.com

Copyright © 2023 Abiodun Rashaun Banjo

All rights reserved.

Paperback ISBN: 979-8-9873836-0-5

Digital ISBN: 979-8-9873836-1-2

Edited by Chelsea Jackson (www.chelsea-jackson.com)

Cover art by: Grip Gurus LLC.

Table of Contents

Foreword..i
Introduction..1
Step 1: Know Yourself..7
Step 2: Set High Expectations...............................17
Step 3: Seek Out the Positive................................23
Step 4: Avoid the Easy Road.................................31
Step 5: Set a Goal..39
Step 6: Be Accountable...55
Step 7: Work Hard Even When No One is Watching........61
Step 8: Stay Resilient..67
Step 9: Grab a Lifeline..73
Step 10: Practice Gratitude...................................79
Conclusion..83
Acknowledgments..85
About the Author..87

Dedication

For my parents, thank you for the unwavering example and standards you provided.

To Shan, when we were 17 years old, you said basketball was only the beginning. You were so right!

To my daughters, may you always remember your greatness.

Foreword

One of the lessons I learned at an early age is that trying to navigate life's travails alone is a nearly impossible task. Had it not been for my father, mother, and other relatives, I can confidently say my life would not be as enriched as it is today. Still, I often wonder, as I wrestle with ways to lift others up, what about those not as fortunate? What about those young boys and girls who do not have the benefit of a father's stern but loving warning, or the wise guiding voice of a mother? What about those that do not have someone reaching back to help them navigate the turbulent waters of this earthly journey? Who will help them?

The pages that follow describe hard-learned lessons around leadership, making difficult decisions, and fostering determination and endurance. These are lessons my friend and colleague Rashaun Banjo has embodied and modeled with courage and generosity. I am remarkably proud of Rashaun for creating this excellent book on mentoring and am grateful for his vulnerability as he shares the knowledge he has gained along his journey. What he has written is a valuable guide for those who ask the same questions I do; who will help those young people who are struggling? And how? If we are honest with ourselves, we know the answer to the first question is found by looking in the mirror. Then, we can pick up Rashaun's book, dig deep, and learn how best to support future generations.

Dr. Jonathan Quash
Executive Director for the CUNY Black Male Initiative
December 2022

Introduction

This book was written by a man raised in an environment of low expectations, one who knows what it's like to be surrounded by that common but false narrative sold to young people of color that says, "You cannot achieve anything and committing your time and energy to reach a goal is pointless." That narrative is not only untrue, it is disempowering and destructive, imposed on entire communities to make them believe they are doomed to fail. For many years I bought into this belief. I would often ask, "Why do I feel like there is nothing for me in the world?" "Why does it seem like success and opportunity come so easily to everyone except me?" If chances did come my way, I would engage in negative self-talk, telling myself, "I'm sure I will find a way to mess this chance up." Like so many young people, I felt set up to fail. This resignation left me disconnected from the opportunities I wanted and detached from the person I hoped to become.

We have to examine why these feelings and self-talk exist. We must question the sense of apathy that can distort young people's outlook and their hope for the future. A deficit mindset is permeating our most vital resource, our youth, and we must act with a sense of urgency. As parents, mentors, teachers, coaches, and youth leaders, we must offer them our support. This goes beyond providing them with the material items we never received as a child. They need lessons, experiences, and role models that empower them to: develop goals, foster their imagination, strengthen their sense of self-worth, and motivate them to act.

The questions and mindset I mentioned above began to change when I started to play basketball. It was on the basketball court that I discovered so much of myself and my potential. The sport, along with its coaches, trainers, and competition, helped me obtain a college education, introduced me to the woman that would become my wife, and instilled within me many of the lessons and concepts I discuss in this book. It's incredible to think the experiences brought on by a round, orange-and-black-striped ball turned a doubtful, self-destructive young man into the person I am today. Still, you don't need to be a coach or sports enthusiast to read and utilize this book, nor do the youth you work with need to be athletes. No matter where you find yourself, this book offers transferable skills and lessons to benefit you and the youth entrusted to your care.

Getting the most out of this book:

The format and layout of this book are intentional. My hope is that by using stories from my personal experience, you can reflect on your own. Many of us have skills and strengths to support our youth; we just need to take time to sift through and identify them. Therefore, I follow each chapter with Mentor Reflections to deepen your self-awareness and leadership skills and assess your own unique wisdom and stories. I also have included Conversation Starters and Action Steps that can be used and adapted for youth. These prompts are my effort to initiate open dialogue, which is crucial to young people's development and the mentoring process.

The foundational belief of this book is that to be successful, everyone must commit to their goals and map out the steps needed to accomplish them. It also understands the role of parents, coaches, teachers, and other role models as vital to the success of our youth. These leaders not only aid children and teens in their journey to success but encourage, teach, and lead by example. We cannot be thoughtful leaders without first doing the internal work ourselves. If our job is to help our youth claim their potential, visualize their goals, and courageously work toward the best versions of themselves, then we must always strive for the best versions of ourselves.

Why Now?

The goal of this book is not to explain the many challenges young people of color face across this country. A research-based text with data, statistics, and a disproportionality analysis would better illustrate these ongoing racial complexities. Instead, this book is a compilation of my personal and professional learnings, observations, experiences, and reflections: a recount of the lessons I have learned throughout my life that apply to the challenges facing many of my younger brothers and sisters. During my fourteen-year career in public education, I watched many students become emotionally disengaged, leaving them further withdrawn from school, their social circles, and their community. This disengagement was further augmented by the recent COVID-19 shutdowns and the switch to remote learning. When students finally did return, they came back more distant, uninterested, and apathetic than ever. This book aims to mitigate such disengagement and support the growth and critical thinking skills necessary for our youth to move from a deficit mindset to a growth mindset.

Through this book, I want our young people to understand that an abundance of opportunities exists for them, including those outside of entertainment and athletics. I want them to believe they can attain countless and varied goals, experiences, and careers. I want them to know that their present situation is not their permanent location. I want to awaken them to the idea that life is a journey and there are people around to help them along the way. I am here to remind my young brothers and sisters that they are truly kings and queens and that greatness lies within them. Unfortunately, many African Americans born in the U.S. feel like opportunities are out-of-reach and limited. While it is true that many systems exist to see us fail, we cannot overlook the agency and opportunities that exist in our own backyard.

I hope that by reading this book, you can support these changes in the young people in your life. Additionally, I hope you see positive impacts in yourself as a mentor and someone with their own hopes and goals, and that you share all you learn with your community. That is how lasting change happens; it ripples outward. In that rippling, may we not just survive in this country; may we thrive and nurture empowered generations. Let's get started.

Step 1: Know Yourself

"Finding yourself is the biggest obstacle…[but] I'm at my best when I'm not in denial of who I am."

– Kendrick Lamar ("97 Seconds" Interview, Hot 97, 2012)

Before a person can truly dig into the principles and practices of success, they must first assess their self-concept and self-efficacy. *Self-concept* refers to the beliefs and images a person holds about their identity, worth, ability, etc. In comparison, *self-efficacy* relates to someone's trust in their ability, knowledge, and capacity to achieve their goals.

Multiple components shape our sense of self. Who we think we are, what we think others expect from us, and who we want to or feel we should be all influence how we view ourselves and understand success. In turn, these views and understandings (i.e., self-concept and self-efficacy) profoundly impact our behaviors and the goals we set. These complex and interrelated factors, combined with the fact that young people's sense of identity is in constant flux, means we must support their growth and ensure they develop their own healthy sense of self.

When I was thirteen, I underwent a significant growth spurt, growing 4 inches over two summers. I can remember the attention I began to attract. Folks started asking me how tall I was or how tall my father was: as if they could foretell my final height. Then came the onslaught of inevitable questions from friends, family, and even strangers. *Are you playing basketball?*

When are you going to sign up for basketball? Do you have a shot? Can you dunk? Are you getting ready for the N.B.A.?

Around this time, I became an active player and fan of the game. But these questions and their implications started to influence my self-concept to the point where I saw myself as a basketball star. I quickly shifted my goals and identity and envisioned playing in high school, getting into a decent college, and maybe playing professionally. Now before this, I had been excited to go into business. I didn't know exactly what industry, but as a kid, I saw guys in suits, and it looked like they did well,

so I was determined to find a career that required a suit. It's funny how quickly the power of suggestion can change you because the next thing I knew, all I wanted to do was to become the best basketball player I could be.

This story leads us to consider the power of suggestion and suggestibility. The American Psychological Association defines *suggestibility* as "an inclination to readily and uncritically adopt the ideas, beliefs, attitudes, or actions of others." Each person has a different level of suggestibility, and it's important to note that suggestibility is different from changing your mind based on new information, learnings, lessons, or growth. It happens when we don't pause to think about how others impact us, our behaviors, and our beliefs, and it can lead us to become someone we don't recognize or resonate with. Many people, including youth, have a high suggestibility. It is how many of us try to gain the approval of our family, friends, peers, and authority figures. But we must have a strong sense of self and personal awareness to know who we are, what values we hold, where we want to end up, and who we will invite to accompany us along the way.

When we are young, we don't always see the full scope of our gifts. We don't consider the many choices we may have or recognize when well-meaning people might be putting us in a box. At the time, I didn't realize growing four inches and playing a sport I enjoyed meant others would assume I could become a professional athlete or that I would adopt that belief, but that's the type of power our words hold. And for those of us parenting, coaching, mentoring, or otherwise working with youth, we must remember the words we speak, and the assumptions we make can wound and confuse young people as fast as they can strengthen and empower them. That is why we must not only be careful about the words we use and the questions we ask, we must also teach young people to have a strong sense of who they are and what they want.

Obtaining and maintaining a strong sense of self is difficult for anyone, and each of us can be overly susceptible to the thoughts, opinions, and actions of others. So how do we help our youth prepare? Well, we first must be safe and respectful places for them to come with their questions, concerns, and wonderings. If we want them to have a strong sense of self, then we can't shut them down when they come to us with something important to them, even if we don't fully understand it.

"We must be safe and respectful places for youth to come with their questions, concerns, and wonderings."

Additionally, we should follow their lead when it comes to their interests and encourage them to pursue passions and set goals that are meaningful to them; that way, we help them grow into the identity and accomplishments they envision. Finally, we check in with them often. We ask questions like: *What do the people around you say or assume about you? How does that* influence or match up to how you see yourself? What do you envision when you think of what you want or are passionate about? Where do you imagine yourself in the future? Does it feel possible? Does it align with your self-concept and passions? Does it align with what others envision for you? What can you do to make your goals happen? What do you need from those around you to accomplish your goals?

For me, basketball is both something that was projected onto me and something I became passionate about. Fortunately, many of those basketball-related goals manifested in my life and led to a sense of personal success. I did attend a prestigious high school and played basketball at a reasonably high level. I accepted a scholarship to attend a private university and even played professionally for a short time. I was and am truly blessed to have lived this athletic experience. However, sometimes I ask myself, *What would have happened if I didn't grow so tall? Would I have been motivated to go into business earlier? Was my community's power of suggestibility so strong that I would have become whatever they told me I should be?*

If people had told me I could be an author rather than a basketball player, maybe I would have written this book sooner. If someone had realized I was good with numbers, they might have inspired me to start a career in finance. I may have dreamt about working on Wall Street instead of dunking hoops.

People, places, and environments help shape the person we become. This means that what youth internalize and how they see themselves influence their future and provide a visual picture of who and what they can become. If they are to be the best versions of themselves, then they must acquire a positive and generative mindset. Creating this type of mindset and an authentic sense of self takes consistency and the courage to develop self-knowledge.

Self-knowledge is knowing oneself, understanding our own mental states, feelings, and thoughts, and being aware of our beliefs, character, motives, and desires. It requires us to continually learn about ourselves, assess how we think, feel, and see the world, and be willing to intentionally and carefully change those perspectives when we get new information. It is vital if we are to consciously choose our path

forward and work mindfully toward our goals and achievements. Conversely, not having a solid sense of self-concept, -efficacy, and -knowledge also impacts one's behavior and future. The only way youth can become successful is to know who they are and believe they are capable and worthy of success.

As leaders and mentors, we are to help guide the youth under our supervision and instill within them a strong sense of self. So how will you positively impact those young people around you? You may not have an answer to that question yet, but by the end of this book, you will have uncovered experiences, lessons, and insights to strengthen your mentorship skills.

Mentor Reflections:

1. When you were growing up, what helped shape your mindset and sense of self? (e.g., What were you praised for? How were your interests received? What did people know or assume about you? What words or other encouragement were you given?)
2. Did these experiences influence your current work or career choice?
3. How would you describe your self-concept? Self-efficacy? Self-knowledge? (Share these with the youth you work with.)

Youth Conversation Starters:

1. What expectations do people have for me? How do these make me feel? Do they align with who I am?
2. What expectations or beliefs do I have about myself? Do my behaviors, actions, and self-concept align with these expectations and beliefs?
3. What are some gifts, interests, and passions I have? Do I envision them playing a role in my future? If so, how?

Step 2: Set High Expectations

"I like the person that you are, but I'm in love with the person that you have potential to be." – Wale ("Ambitious Girl," 2010)

My mother always said my siblings and I were going to college. It wasn't negotiable or even a big topic of conversation. Instead, it was mentioned as if it was akin to going to the dentist or a doctor's appointment, casually and matter-of-fact. So as children, we never really had any other way to think of ourselves except as college-educated or college-eligible because it was the only option, a mandatory future route instilled upon and accepted by us at an early age.

I understand why my mother expected college education to be mandatory. At that time, the rate of African American males entering college or university was even lower than it is now. For her, a college education was not a luxury; it was a form of empowerment, a vital component of our futures. She went to great lengths to ensure we believed in our own ability and intelligence and that we took responsibility for our success. She took us to museums, immersed us in cultural experiences, ensured we completed summer book reports, and consistently reminded us that we could enter any sector, career, or industry we wanted. Fast forward to today, and all three of us have bachelor's degrees, while two of us went on to master-level programs.

The moral of the story is that, in many cases, with the proper support and frameworks, we rise to the expectations set for us. The standard of excellence we hold for our young people doesn't set them up to fail; it pushes them toward success. My mom's expectations of the youth in her household created a college culture in our home. The culture she built was so strong that it has spanned generations, and years later, when my younger cousin came to live with us, I set the same standard and culture for her. She now has a bachelor's and a master's degree.

However, one thing I do lament is that I didn't see a college campus until I became a serious athlete and received basketball scholarship offers. And when I did start looking at colleges, I  thought my experience would be like Jesus Shuttlesworth's in the movie *He Got Game*, where I'd be highly sought after and recruited by multiple schools. Like most youth, I envisioned and emulated what I saw in entertainment, so at that time, all I knew about what it meant to be a Black college student came from sports-centered movies like *The Program* and shows like *A Different World.*

Times have changed since my own college experience. Youth now have far more information and access, and can take virtual tours and connect with students, faculty, and staff to learn about the opportunities ahead of them. But what hasn't changed is the need for young people to articulate and envision their success. We can't just tell youth what they are capable of; we must show them and consistently affirm that they are valuable and worthy of our investment and support.

Within my work, when a student shows interest in a particular subject, sport, club, or career, we challenge them to learn more about it and help them imagine where following that passion may lead. For example, several young players at Team Crate Hoops showed interest in attending private high schools. Together with their families they set this goal, and our role was to prepare them for the experience. Academically, we supported test preparation for the specialized

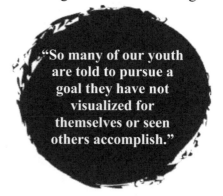

"So many of our youth are told to pursue a goal they have not visualized for themselves or seen others accomplish."

entrance exams. We also introduced them to faculty, staff, coaches, and families from those schools and physically took them on campus visits so they could experience the schools firsthand. As a result, not only did many of the players earn entrance due to their basketball skills, but all of them were also academically eligible for acceptance. Through this preparation, each of the students and their families learned that you have to change your mindset and hone your vision if you want to obtain a goal.

So many of our youth are told to pursue a goal they have not visualized for themselves or seen others accomplish. This makes it hard for them to feel connected to or fully invested in their success. If the young people you work with want to attend college, bring them to a university. If they are interested in a particular career, take them to a workplace within that sector; let them be immersed in the experience and really see themselves there. Introduce them to people with valuable experience and knowledge they can learn from. Take the youth you work with to the places they want to grow into, and then help them map the path to getting there. We can't accompany them on their path to success if we aren't helping them glimpse what the destination might look like.

Mentor Reflections:

1. When you were growing up, did you have a clear vision of your goals or where you wanted to end up? Why or why not?
2. What support did you have or would have liked to have to help solidify your vision and work toward your goals?
3. What goals do you have for yourself now, and how do you envision, experience, or learn about your hoped-for destination?

Youth Conversation Starters:

1. Think about one goal you have. Envision what reaching that goal might look and feel like. Describe what you see.
2. What questions do you have about your goal or the destination you see for yourself? Who can help you answer those questions?
3. What firsthand experiences may help you better achieve your goal?

Step 3: Seek Out the Positive

"I believe that the energy you put out in the world, you get back." – Jay-Z

When I was a college athlete, we would always eat chicken parmesan before game day. Over the years, I ate so much of it that I rarely eat it today. Still, the reason we ate the same meal over and over wasn't to bore us; instead, it was to fill our bodies with as many nutrients, carbohydrates, and proteins as we could for the upcoming game. This routine taught me to be intentional about what I consume, and I take this lesson into my daily life. Not only do I apply that rule to what I eat, but I am also conscious about the television shows I watch, the music I listen to, and most importantly, the people I am around.

It's no secret that technology has advanced our way of communicating with, accessing, and viewing the world. At any given moment, we can google questions our grandparents never even thought to ask and connect to people halfway across the world through apps, games, and social media. Each day we are bombarded with thousands of ads and get constant notifications from twenty-four-hour news cycles. Growing up, I remember my T.V. channel options were 2, 9, 11, and 76; now, we have streaming sites with endless content, so much so that we can spend an hour just looking for a show to watch.

These realities are both a blessing and a curse. Sure, we can virtually tour a museum in France or tune into a live video of the International Space Station as it orbits the planet. But, we can also consume media, music, and comment sections that add little value to our life. Carefully and mindfully processing the deluge of content, businesses, entertainers, news outlets, and politicians fighting for our attention is nearly impossible, and it's not something humans were made to do, including young people.

Our youth are overwhelmed with a constant barrage of facts, knowledge, opinions, and events, and have little skills to wade through all that information with intentionality, wisdom, and a healthy dose of suspicion. In a crucial stage of their identity formation and the development of their critical thinking skills, they are sold thousands of marketed perceptions of themselves, others, and the world each day.

However, with some intentionality and patience, we can help youth create their own filters, teach them how to identify the messages they are receiving, and assess how those messages positively or negatively impact them.

Even if you aren't a Spiderman fan, you are probably familiar with the popular saying, "With great power comes great responsibility." This responsibility applies to what media and information we choose to ingest. Technology, art, and media are powerful forces, but we are also powerful and can choose what we do with these tools. As a mentor, are you seeking things that add positive value to your life or those that focus on, perpetuate, and engrain the negative? What about the youth you work with?

One example is the music we listen to. I am a fan of Hip Hop. Growing up in Southeast Queens, I resonated with the stories and lives of rappers like Nas and Mobb Deep and experienced the youthful injustices and constant struggle that many artists of that era rapped about. However, music is rapidly changing, and not all of it is for the better. We have to be careful about what messages youth are allowing themselves to be exposed to. I often challenge the young people I work with to think of their favorite Hip Hop song. I ask them: *Would you want your mom listening to that song? Would you want your younger siblings or cousins to bop to that tune? If you had kids, would you want them to sing the lyrics with you?* If they answer "no" to any of these, I encourage them to consider the energy and value systems they allow into their lives. These conversations are also a good reminder that if we engage in music, media, and lifestyles that are uncomfortable for us to talk about, share, or experience with our community, then they might not be good for us.

"We can't expect positivity, growth, and success to come from negative energies and sources."

I mentioned earlier that we would eat chicken parmesan to fuel our bodies for the game ahead. One of the reasons this was so important for me is because, at that age, I didn't have great eating habits. I would often eat takeout and put other unhealthy foods in my body. Eating a more balanced meal helped ensure I was ready to perform my best, and who knows how my performance would have improved had I been consistent with feeding my body better. Either way, we can't expect positivity, growth, and success to come from negative energies and sources. If youth don't intentionally consume value-added social media, music, entertainment, podcasts, and books, how will they have the support, energy, and information needed to pursue their goals?

Who we are is a mixture of who we surround ourselves with, the influences we intake, and the habits we form. We must continually assess the information we are taking in and compare it to who we are and what we want to put into the world.

Mentor Reflections:

1. What music, movies, books, shows, etc., did you consume when you were younger? Why? How did they make you feel? Looking back, would you choose differently?
2. What sources of information and entertainment do you engage with today? How do these help you be a better mentor and leader?

Youth Action Steps:

1. Open your social media apps and do a quick inventory. Who are you following? Why? What are the common themes of the influencers and accounts you follow, and do they align with your values? If not, consider unfollowing them.
2. Take an inventory of the information that you're absorbing. What are the shows you watch, the music you listen to, and the things you read? Do the lifestyles, values, and lessons from those sources align with who you want to be in ten years?

3. List 2-3 current behaviors that don't align with your overall values and goals. Why do you behave in that way? Who/what around you reinforces those behaviors, and how can you decrease their impact on your life?

Step 4: Avoid the Easy Road

"You have to keep your vision clear, cause only a coward lives in fear." – Nas ("Friends," 2010)

Rarely is the easy road the best road, and rarely does the fastest option lead to the best long-term success. I learned this lesson when I got to college. I had the typical freshman experience, getting acclimated to the campus, registering for classes, and figuring out what it meant to live away from home. A fellow teammate and I were both freshmen from the city and followed a similar trajectory. We lived in the same dorm, chose the same major, and matched our schedules to ensure we made it to basketball practice on time. So early in our first year, it was no surprise that we walked into an auditorium sectioned off by major, and both decided to major in business. We didn't know what we wanted to do, but business seemed like a path to money, and of course, like many people, we wanted to go to school, get a degree, and get straight to making money. However, we quickly learned that the Business Program threw students right into the deep end of mathematics, management, administration, and economics courses. It became immediately apparent that we weren't in high school anymore, and our grades took a hit that first semester.

"Rarely is the easy road the best road, and rarely does the fastest option lead to the best long-term success."

Not only were we navigating a higher academic level, but we were still getting used to a rigorous basketball schedule and learning what it meant to be a serious college-level athlete (which, for those who don't know, is similar to having a full-time job). So, after that first semester, we were inching closer to academic probation and needed to clean up our grades. Someone suggested we change our majors to something that required fewer math and science courses to decrease our workload. Now, my teammate was all for that solution. Many of our teammates and fellow student-athletes majored in Communications or sports-related degrees, partly because the workload for those majors felt more manageable. When my teammate decided to change his major, I strongly considered doing the same, but I knew I wasn't interested in those subjects.

So, I was faced with a choice; take on a major that, for me, felt unexciting and like an easy out, or continue to challenge myself and go for the major I wanted to succeed in. To help me with my decision, I reached out to my former high school basketball coach for some much-needed advice. We methodically went through the options and weighed the pros and cons of each. It was all helpful, but the most meaningful thing he said in our conversation was, "the tough thing about taking the easy road is that it becomes a habit." I still carry that reminder with me to this day.

Many of us come to crossroads where we can choose either the easy solution or the one that will push us closer to what we truly want. The thing is, when we choose the former, we don't give ourselves the opportunity to strengthen our skills or build resiliency. We also risk making a habit out of taking the easy road. Each time we betray what we want and choose what is fastest or most accessible, we make it more difficult to make hard choices in the future.  If we do this too much, we can end up discouraged and shut down when faced with any challenge, or we may become confused and frustrated because we aren't as successful as we'd like.

As you might imagine, I did continue with my business degree. However, I had to make changes, decisions, and sacrifices to succeed in that major. I altered some of my social habits, regularly attended study hall, and utilized each of my professors' office hours to get extra time and help from them. As a result, I successfully graduated with a Bachelor's in Business and remained a strong student-athlete throughout my four years in college. The work I had to put in was not easy or for the faint of heart, but not only do I have the knowledge and skills I needed to succeed in the business sector, I also have confidence and a pride in myself that no one can take away.

It's so vital that we challenge ourselves and not back down or take the easy way out. It's equally important that we model and instill this trait in our youth. Foresight is not a strength young people are known to have. Developmentally, it can be difficult for them to see and understand long-term consequences and action steps. But as my former basketball coach demonstrated, our job is not to force their hand in decision-making but to help them see where each crossroad might lead them and assist them in planning accordingly.

Additionally, we must empathize with them in their decision-making. There are many reasons someone might take what seems to be an "easy way out." Maybe they aren't truly passionate about the goal at the end of the difficult road, maybe their interests really do lie elsewhere, or perhaps they've never been told they can persevere in the face of challenges. The young people we work with must know they can do the hard things and that fear of failing or making a mistake should never prevent them from walking the path they want to be on.

I'm constantly reminding the youth I work with that if they really want something, they have to work, problem-solve, and create solutions that best serve them and their goal. Of course, it's normal to want to run from challenges or find the fastest answers, but in most cases, they will be less fulfilling or their destinations less meaningful. Most of all, when we choose the easy road just to avoid the pain, uncertainty, and sacrifice of hard work, we shortchange ourselves of the lessons, growth, and strength those challenges offer.

> "When we choose the easy road just to avoid the pain, uncertainty, and sacrifice of hard work, we shortchange ourselves of the lessons, growth, and strength those challenges offer."

Mentor Reflections:

1. Is there a challenge you avoided in the past? Why did you avoid it? Share your story/experience with the youth you work with.
2. What is a past challenge you faced head-on and put in the hard work to achieve? How did you feel once you reached your goal? Share your story/experience with the youth you work with.

Youth Conversation Starters:

1. What do you do when faced with a challenge? Are there any practices, tools, or people that would make facing challenges easier for you?
2. Who do you go to if you need help making a big decision? Why do you go to them?
3. What considerations do you think through when faced with a decision? Why?

Step 5: Set a Goal

"Every day is a new opportunity to reach [your] goal."

– Rick Ross

Most people don't get in a car without knowing where they are going. Similar to identifying a travel destination, goals are our way of intentionally dropping a G.P.S. pin and giving our lives some direction. There can be different methods, approaches, and layers to setting goals, but simply put, they are where we want to end up. It's concerning to me that many people wake up each day without something they are working towards, something that will help carry them through that day and onto the next. Without a destination, a journey can feel like aimless wandering, and life without a goal can feel the same.

"Similar to identifying a travel destination, goals are our way of intentionally dropping a G.P.S. pin and giving our lives some direction."

In 2006, I accepted a contract to play professional basketball in a small area of Portugal called Torres Novas. It wasn't known for having the best basketball league, but I didn't want to be home and was happy to have the opportunity to continue playing. I stayed in a relatively nice residential area with apartment buildings, small family homes, decent schools, and several grocery stores. However, I felt completely isolated. The culture shock, the language barrier, and the fact that it rained for half the year left me depressed. I knew I had to do something to keep my mind from focusing on the negative, so I decided to use my isolation to get better at basketball.

At first, it was weird because most of the team followed the same routine. We would begrudgingly walk to practice together, go to lunch and complain the entire time, and then unenthusiastically head back to practice. But I started to do things differently. Determined to improve my game, I pretended I was in some overseas basketball boot camp and set goals and milestones for myself. For example, I began waking up earlier, getting more shots in before and after practice, and, crucially, changing my mindset. After a week of this shift, I noticed a change in my game and my attitude. Soon, I was charting my days and finding ways to increase my productivity, all so I could improve my skill and decrease my melancholy. But it wasn't enough to keep my body moving; I realized I also had to keep my mind active, so I started reading more, digging into financial literacy and self-help books, as well as biographies and memoirs. Reading consistently wasn't easy at first, but as I kept at it, I realized its importance. Immersing myself in the information, experiences, and thoughts of others eased my loneliness and empowered me to think in new and different ways. These action steps allowed me to meet my personal and professional goals and improved my quality of life as I navigated a new place, culture, and routine.

Fast-forward to today, and I have observed many young people become goalless after the isolation of the pandemic. The lack of a consistent in-person school routine, combined with the distance and loneliness felt by so many, left a large number of students feeling defeated and shut down. To be sure, the pandemic caused a great deal of loss and pain, and it will take us time to heal and rebuild ourselves and our communities, but I'm confident we can. Each of us can do anything we set our mind to, but our minds must first be set on something. That is where the goals come in.

Any goal, whatever goal it is, must be S.M.A.R.T. This common acronym outlines the unique elements vital to any attainable goal; they are:

- S – Specific
- M – Measurable
- A – Attainable
- R – Realistic
- T – Time-bound

Below are descriptions and examples of each component, along with questions you might ask the youth with whom you work.

Specific:

What exactly do you hope to accomplish? How? Why? Who will be involved in helping you reach your goal? Will there be a specific place or places where you will work toward your goal? These types of questions help us hone our goals and add some much-needed specificity. Goals must be specific because if they are too broad, it becomes difficult to move forward. For example, if my goal is "to build wealth," that's a lofty, vague, and broad goal. It does not specify how I might attain wealth or why that goal is important to me. It also doesn't define what "wealth" means to me. But what if my goal is to "create generational and communal wealth by building my own real estate business so I may increase my investments and retire early." Now that is more specific. In this new goal, I am telling myself and everyone around me that I plan to move in a very particular direction and why.

This goal also addresses the "how" by naming the methods I will use to achieve it: building a business and investing. Having these outlined gives me explicit steps to take as I work toward my goal (e.g., studying for and taking the real estate exam, shadowing real estate agents, reading investment books, etc.). Think of specificity as a goal's guardrails. When driving on a winding road, the railing and lines help keep the car on track so it can move toward its destination. Specific goals are the same way.

Measurable:

How will you know when you have reached your goal? How will you track your progress to see if you are close to the finish line or still have far to go? Without measurement tools, we won't know if we're on track to reach our goal or if our current actions aren't working. It can be exhausting and disheartening to find out too late that the things you were doing to reach your goal aren't making the impact you thought, and you now have to go back to the drawing board. This is why it's crucial to identify how you will measure your goals and track your progress. For example, when I played professional basketball, I realized I played better when I devoted extra time to shooting and watching film. Over time I developed a formula; if I shot an extra 1000 shots throughout the week, there was a higher chance I'd have a good game. So I decided to shoot an additional 250 shots before/after practice to reach 1000 per week.

As you can see, I created a way to measure my progress. My goal was to perform better in each game. I defined what that looked like for me and observed the changes I needed to implement to make it happen; then, I put in the work. Though the specific measurements will look different depending on the goal, setting up ways to assess and evaluate our efforts is imperative if we are to succeed.

Attainable:

Is your goal within reach? What resources do you need to achieve it, and can you obtain them? Do you need help to accomplish this goal, or can you reach it by yourself? If our goals are too big, or we try to do too much too fast, then we may not have all the resources we need to succeed. Limited resources, time, and energy are okay and, in fact, are often a reality when we are just starting. However, many people never move past this stage of goal development because it relies on pausing to examine what they do have. If they don't feel they have what they need, then they stop working toward the goal instead of finding a workaround.

I advise you to take stock of your *assets*, or the resources, support, knowledge, and experts you may have access to. Create a starting point from there. Maybe it means you have a short-term goal you must reach before moving toward a bigger one, or you have to scale your plan down a bit to better reflect the time, energy, and resources you have right now. For example, if my goal is to own a car, I should first have a driver's license. This means I need to make time to study and practice for the test before I focus too much on what car to buy. The same approach applies to many of our goals.

Realistic:

This stage requires even more self-reflection. How important is this goal to you? How much time, energy, and sacrifice are you reasonably able and willing to give to it? What other responsibilities, hobbies, or relationships do you have that take your time and attention? A goal is only realistic if we are willing to be real! To use the previous example of buying a car, buying and driving a vehicle is not practical if you don't have a driver's license. Driving the car depends on other preceding steps; before those happen, it is unrealistic to think you can buy and drive a car. Goals require action, so be clear about what action steps you can realistically and consistently achieve, and try to avoid focusing on goals that are too big or may require too much of you too soon.

Another common pitfall is rushing our goals. For example, if my goal is to learn four new languages in one year, chances are I'm setting myself up to fail because I'm not taking into account the time and work needed to do the work successfully. Impatience is natural, but if we don't ensure our goal's scope and time frame are realistic, we are setting ourselves up for disappointment.

Lastly, comparison and competition are additional potential pitfalls when setting realistic goals. The successes of others can be helpful examples and can keep us motivated, but we can also get caught up in chasing a goal that isn't ours. Additionally, we can lose appreciation for our individual gifts, abilities, and capabilities and forget why our goal mattered to us in the first place. Ultimately, you want to do your best without worrying too much about others. These pitfalls can lead to frustration, disillusionment, or giving up altogether. Still, if we learn to work toward realistic and sometimes smaller goals, we will not only succeed but also save ourselves anger, time, and energy.

Time-Bound:

When do you plan on starting and ending your goal? How long do you think it will take you? What consistent time are you able to give to achieve it? Simply put, we must make a timeline for our goal. It should have a start and end date, as well as an outline of milestones we plan to reach and when. These critical components help us break down our goals to feel more manageable and provide parameters to help keep us on track. For example, if my goal is to make $100,000 in a year, that gives me a timeline of 12 months. I can further break that goal into smaller milestones to determine how much I need to make per month. In other words, I would have to make at least $8,335 ($100,000 divided by 12 months) to meet my goal. If I know this, then each month, I can set aside time to track my progress and make adjustments if needed.

A goal without a timeline is like driving a car without knowing how much gas you have; you can be headed in the right direction, but you don't know how far you'll make it or when you will get to your destination. And timelining does not only consider the amount of time needed to complete a goal but also requires you to think about when you can put in the work. What are the consistent blocks of time you plan to work toward your goal? How can you protect that time so you don't get distracted or pulled into something else when you should be working?

Goal Mapping Tools:

Intentionally setting goals can feel overwhelming and complicated for both youth and their mentors. The S.M.A.R.T framework outlined above is designed to simplify the process and provide tangible steps for you to use. Additionally, there are other tools you can use to help you build off of the S.M.A.R.T. framework. I've listed some below. Feel free to research and use any of these if/when you are ready to dive deeper into goal setting.

- **Goals, Objectives, and Activities** – A simple outline of the goal(s) you want to achieve, the objectives that fall under each goal, and the activities or milestones you will engage in to reach success. Remember, each objective and milestone should directly relate to your goal somehow.

- **Micro Goals** – Setting smaller goals that lead to achieving the larger, primary goal. This process can help you keep forward momentum and motivation.
- **Mind Mapping** – A non-linear diagram that visually links tasks, concepts, activities, and other key elements around a central concept (in this case your goal).
- **SWOT Analysis** – SWOT stands for Strengths, Weaknesses, Opportunities, and Threats (e.g., challenges or barriers that may keep you from achieving your goal). By analyzing these four components, you take stock of your assets and opportunities, and prepare yourself for any challenges that may lie ahead.
- **Vision Board** – Creating a collage of words and images (digitally or on paper) that envisions what you hope to accomplish, what you need to meet that goal, and what success will feel/look like.

Most people don't start a journey without a destination, but that is exactly how we live our lives if we do not have well-thought-out goals. As youth begin envisioning and mapping out their future, S.M.A.R.T. goals and the other tools listed above can provide them with the framework to build a plan. These plans can empower them to live into their unique purpose and experience ultimate happiness and fulfillment.

Mentor Reflections:

1. What goal do you have for yourself as a youth leader? Is your goal S.M.A.R.T.? If not, try to reframe it to fit the S.M.A.R.T. framework.
2. What part of the S.M.A.R.T. framework is most difficult for you? Why? What tools or practices might you put in place to overcome this difficulty?
3. Is there a specific Goal Mapping Tool you are interested in learning more about? If so, take some time to do research on it.
4. What is one goal you succeeded at? What helped you be successful? (Share your example with the youth you work with.)

Youth Action Steps:

1. Using the S.M.A.R.T. approach, write the following:
    a. One short-term goal (e.g., something you can achieve daily, weekly, etc. Example: I will make my bed every morning.)

    b. One mid-term goal (e.g., a goal that will take a bit more time. Example: By the end of the year, I will pass all of my classes with a B average.)

    c. One long-term goal (e.g., a goal a little farther out in the future. Example: In five years, I will be a senior in college studying Biology.)

2. What do you do when you feel unmotivated to work toward your goals?
3. What part of the S.M.A.R.T. framework is most difficult for you? Why? What tools or practices might you put in place to overcome this difficulty?

Step 6: Be Accountable

"It's the one thing you can control. You are responsible for how people remember you– or don't. So don't take it lightly." – Kobe Bryant at his jersey retirement press conference on December 18, 2017

As the oldest of three kids, I grew up with a strong sense of responsibility. While my parents worked, I watched out for my siblings, making sure no one burned the house down or got hurt. However, it wasn't until college that I learned what being fully responsible for myself looked like. It was a new, exciting, and terrifying feeling, and learning self-accountability took time and maturity. My harshest lesson came when I arrived late for a college practice. When I lived on campus, I was always with my teammates, so I didn't miss many team functions. However, in my senior year, I moved off campus and was entirely responsible for myself and my time. I had to get up to go to classes and drive myself to practice and games.

One morning I overslept and got to the gym about 10 minutes after practice started. I ran to get dressed; no one was in the locker room. I ran to the court; no one was there. As I looked around, wondering what to do, I saw an assistant coach walking into the film room. He looked at me and shook his head in disappointment. I considered just packing up and going home. I knew I was dead, but I forced myself to walk into that room. Sure enough, right when I entered, the coach laid into me, and my teammates started whispering about me. I have never been cursed out that much in my life. What was worse, I was supposed to be a leader of the team. My tardiness not only set a bad example, but in that moment, it changed how my teammates saw me. I was never late a practice again, and I still carry that lesson with me. We are all accountable to our commitments, our communities, and ourselves, and there are consequences when we don't meet those responsibilities.

Teaching anyone accountability is a difficult task, especially youth. For young people, the consequences of irresponsibility are not as severe as for adults. For example, as an adult, if you don't pay your electric bills, you'll be sitting in the dark. Or if you don't show up to work ready to

> "Teaching responsibility when the stakes are low builds young people's confidence and strengthens their sense of accountability."

contribute to the team, you may be out of a job. Rightfully, the stakes are lower for youth. They shouldn't have to worry about these things yet, and they should have room to make mistakes. In fact, mistakes are a part of growing up, so we should provide space for missteps. However, accountability is still a vital lesson.

Often, youth that are not held accountable become irresponsible adults. Sharing our own lessons and stories, as I have throughout this book, is great. Still, they must also be given concrete, age-appropriate opportunities to practice responsibility if they are going to internalize these lessons. Teaching responsibility when the stakes are low builds their confidence and strengthens their sense of accountability. This then leads to more responsible adults who understand that the thing they can best control is themselves. As adults, we should be modeling accountability and responsible behavior, and challenging our youth to become increasingly accountable for their actions, behaviors, and words. One thing I value is giving youth chores, as chores are one of the first chances youth have to practice responsibility and work for something beyond themselves. Making the bed and taking out the garbage may seem like minor activities in practice. However, the skills and consistency needed for these actions build accountability and teach youth that their responsibility can improve and support their family, community, and the world.

Chores and other forms of responsibility also increase a young person's confidence and self-efficacy. In my work, I often hear youth and mentors say they *can't* do something or that they *don't have what it takes* to reach their goal. In these moments, I have to remind them that their speech has power. Just like how we speak to others matters, how we speak to (and about) ourselves is very important. Our words can break us down or raise us up. They can reframe how we see ourselves and our abilities. If we tell ourselves we can't do something before we even start, then we've already washed our hands of responsibility and set ourselves up for defeat. This leads to a cycle of self-fulfilling prophecies, where the young person believes they can't do something and effectively denounces all personal accountability. As a result, they don't put in the energy or work and, unsurprisingly, don't accomplish what they already believed they couldn't do. To address this self-defeating language and the mentality behind it, I encourage my youth to start their sentences with "I can…" or "I am capable…" A lot of our youth need to hear this from themselves and us if they are to believe they are responsible and capable; otherwise, they won't see any point in accountability.

Mentor Reflections:

1. In what ways do you hold yourself accountable? How do you ensure that you're consistent in meeting the behaviors and actions required of you?
2. What are age-appropriate ways to foster accountability and increase confidence in the youth you work with?

Youth Conversation Starters:

1. How do you define accountability and responsibility? Why are they important?
2. Who do you feel accountable to (e.g., parents, family, teammates, teachers, etc.)? What do you do to demonstrate your accountability?

Step 7: Work Hard Even When No One is Watching

"The hardest thing to do is work hard when no one is watching." – Ray Lewis

In my senior year of high school, I was nominated for the McDonald's All American Game and joined the All-Long Island basketball team. I also played in the Wheelchair Classic—a massive charity game that brought together all of NYC's top talent—and was invited to join the city's best to compete against Chicago in the Windy City Classic. I was honored to be a part of these opportunities, yet I also felt I belonged in those spaces. In these all-star settings, I recognized I could hold my own among my teammates and competitors, and that my hard work was getting put to good use.

My high school basketball coach, one of my biggest supporters to this day, came with me to Chicago for the Classic. During our trip, he took me to my first professional basketball game, where the Bulls played the Charlotte Hornets. I remember we got to the game early so I could watch the warmups. It was a lesson in hard work I will never forget.

I watched a big name at that time, Eddie Jones, warmup. He was one of my favorite players, and I took on many of his moves. Being 6'6 and lanky, he had a frame similar to mine. As I watched him warm up, I couldn't believe how focused he was. This was twenty minutes before the game, and this guy was making every jump shot—left dribble, right dribble, double cross, *swoosh*, nothing but net. I had never seen a pro before. We all watch games on T.V., but watching a professional in person is different. So as Jones was warming up, hitting shot after shot, it occurred to me, he wasn't even starting that night. Here was this guy, putting in all kinds of work right before a game, and he wasn't even going to be in the spotlight when the game started. When I looked at it that way, I realized I had no excuse not to put in the hard work. Players like Jones and other legends may have inherent talent, but they also put in an incredible amount of time, energy, and effort. So much work happens before we watch pros like them dominate in a game, and it's not just about how much they practice; it's about their lifestyle. It's about how they care for themselves, how much sleep they get, what they put into their body, how they relate to their loved ones; all of that impacts their success in their sport and their lives as a whole.

So much of our world is dependent on convenience and speed. From microwaves and 5G devices to overnight shipping and getting social media likes, we want things done quickly and easily. We crave that instant gratification and attention, and then when we get it, we rush off to find more. But having things come fast and easy can not only make us a bit lazy, it can decrease our capacity for patience, inconvenience, and consistent work. Having everything right away can also overshadow the actual work and the people that go into making things look effortless. As a result, we only see part of the picture, the end result, instead of everything it took to get there. That night at the game, I wasn't seeing the tens of thousands of hours those pros put into their craft or the work of the coaches, managers, and referees who made that game possible. I didn't see all the sacrifices the players made to get to where they were at that moment, playing in front of a high school student and a sold-out crowd. I just saw the result of their sacrifice.

"Having things come fast and easy can decrease our capacity for patience, inconvenience, and consistent work."

At that game, I asked myself how hard I was willing to work and what I was willing to sacrifice to pursue my goals in basketball. Whether the youth we work with have sports-related goals or not, the lesson and questions are the same. We should be asking our young people: *What amount of energy and dedication is needed for you to be successful? What are you willing to sacrifice to meet your goal? What are you willing to risk? Are you willing to be patient and do the long, hard, unseen work?*

And like my coach did with me, we should encourage our youth to watch those they want to become. Do they want to be a doctor, a producer, a soccer player, a rapper? They should find people in those fields and pay attention to the work they do, how they act, and the sacrifices they make behind the scenes when no one is watching. Our youth should learn from them and determine if they are prepared to patiently commit to the skill-building, self-care, and sacrifice needed to accomplish their goals. If not, they risk not being able to reach their full potential.

Mentor Reflections:

1. When you were growing up, who did you admire? Why? Did you learn anything about hard work and dedication from them? If so, what?
2. What sacrifices have you made to reach your goals? Share your story/experience with the youth you work with.

Youth Action Steps:

1. Identify at least two people who have achieved success or a goal you want to achieve and who share similar values to you. Learn as much about their routine, their lifestyle, their dedication, and the discipline they have developed to achieve success. Also, learn what they do when they inevitably fall short or fail. (You can do this research using social media, interviews, articles, etc.)
2. What are two tangible practices you might implement into your own life and routine to help you meet one of your goals?

Step 8: Stay Resilient

"Everyone's got a plan until you get punched in the face." – Mike Tyson

Merriam-Webster defines *resiliency* as "an ability to recover from or adjust easily to adversity or change." It's a word we hear about often, and it can mean different things to different people. Yet one thing is for sure, big or small, we all face challenges or adversities in our lives. Even if you have a plan, a vision board, a five-year timeline, a bucket list, etc., obstacles and upsets can arise anytime. Being resilient will ensure you can withstand just about anything that comes your way. However, just like a muscle, resiliency is built; it is a conscious practice that requires skill and experience.

"Just like a muscle, resiliency is built; it is a conscious practice that requires skill and experience."

In 2004, I had a contract to travel to Luxembourg (a small country bordering Germany) for my first opportunity to play professional basketball. Upon arriving, I learned that instead of automatically joining the team, I would have a tryout that lasted two weeks, where I would compete with another American for one position. I took this challenge head-on because I certainly did not want to return home. I had just told everyone in my community that I'd be playing professional basketball, not going to a tryout. So I trained hard, and after two weeks, the other

American player and I were ready. But, unfortunately, in the end, they didn't choose me. I was devastated. I was sent back home after one unsuccessful try and felt like a complete failure. It felt like everything I had hoped and prepared for would never come to pass. So, I stayed home for a couple of weeks, moved around, and started a regular nine-to-five job which I actually enjoyed. But my true passion and desire to play didn't die.

One day I was outside just working out and playing with some of the guys when a passing colleague asked me, "Why are you still here?" Confused, I asked him what he meant. He responded, "The way you're playing, you have the ability to play at a high level, so why are you limiting yourself?" His inquiry baffled me, and at that moment, I realized I had let one adversity stop me from pursuing my goal and doing something I loved.

And so, for the next four weeks, I dedicated everything I could to training and getting back in shape so that I could play at the highest level possible. Within the next month and a half, I was flying overseas to Turkey for another tryout. As you might have guessed from the story in section five, this tryout was successful, and I continued a four-year career playing in several different countries. Through this experience, I learned resiliency is not about perfection or never failing; it's about having the inner strength, endurance, and flexibility to learn from our shortfalls and using those learnings as fuel toward the next goal.

There will be times when our youth fall or make mistakes. After all, we all have fallen short of our goals or of the person we hoped to be. When we fall, we should take a minute, do what we need to do to take care of ourselves, and reflect. But true power is getting back up. That's the message we should be repeating for our youth. They should know that as long as they get back up, they didn't fail; they just learned a lesson. It's when we don't get back up that our mistake turns into a failure. Failure is inaction; it is getting comfortable with less than our best. Through our patience and encouragement, our youth should come to see mistakes as lessons to apply in the future. This is how they build resilience.

I've learned so much about resilience from my two daughters. As I watched them learn to walk, never in their 100 falls did they say, "Well, walking isn't for me." or "These legs aren't meant to work." No, they kept trying until they mastered the skill. That determination to learn, regardless of the outcome or instant gratification of success, enlightened me. Giving up is a learned skill; we are born resilient. We are born naturally unaware of the limitations placed on us, the ones that convince us we can't do something. So if we can learn to quit, we can relearn to be resilient.

As mentors and youth leaders, we have to be comfortable with our personal shortcomings, and we must model getting back up. We must demonstrate grace, patience,

> "If we can learn to quit, we can relearn to be resilient."

determination, and resilience for ourselves and others. Additionally, we must honestly share stories and experiences of our mistakes and lessons. When we do this, our youth will understand that when they fall: they can take a second, they can be disappointed and frustrated, they can even make adjustments to their plans, goals, and timelines, but they should always get back up.

Mentor Reflections:

1. What challenges have you faced that tested and strengthened your resilience? Share a story/experience with the youth you work with.
2. When you make a mistake or things don't go as you envisioned, what skills, practices, and tools do you use to get back up and try again? Consider sharing those with the youth you work with.

Youth Conversation Starters:

1. Think about a time you were faced with an unexpected obstacle or challenge. How did you overcome it, and how did that feel? What did it teach you?
2. Consider a current obstacle or challenge you might be encountering. What past lessons, practices, or tools might help you face it?

Step 9: Grab a Lifeline

"Well, from my understanding, people get better when they start to understand that they are valuable."
– Mos Def ("Fear Not of Man," 1999)

In the popular game show *Who Wants to Be a Millionaire*, if the contestant cannot correctly answer a question, they can seek help by using one of their three "lifelines." These lifelines can be family, friends, strangers, and even the audience, who can advise them on which trivia answer to select. The contestant decides when to use this opportunity, and many use it when a question completely stumps them. Often, lifelines lead to the contestant choosing the correct answer and progressing further in the game. This example reminds us that everyone needs help, and we all have lifelines we can reach out to. It's important to know who our lifelines are and how we can keep them close, especially in times of need.

I have been blessed to have many people willing to help and support me, especially my mother, who has been one of my closest role models and personal advisors. There have been occasions where her wisdom has shown me a different perspective and allowed me to better understand how I am impacting my environment and those around me. At their best, that's what mentors and role models do; expand how we see the world and help us better understand our place in it. They do this by stretching our perspectives, fostering our skills, challenging us to think critically, and encouraging us to improve.

For many of us (and our youth), our initial role models are our parents. Ideally, they are the first ones who provide the love, security, and guidance we need. However, sometimes our parents are not our primary role models. Maybe an aunt, uncle, grandparent, or someone else entirely fulfills that role for us. The point is that no matter our circumstances, there are usually people around us that we can depend on, people who make us better. If they are not immediately in our households, we may have to look elsewhere, and though that may be frustrating and painful, it is vital that we have mentors, especially during pivotal times in our growth and development.

Often teachers, coaches, or community members serve as role models for our youth, and sometimes mentorship does not come from just one person, as different mentors offer different things. But no matter what, one of the keys to working with youth is to be genuine. Young people can sense when adults are inauthentic or patronizing, leading to mistrust or opposition. Instead, when mentoring, bring your authentic (and best) self and trust that young people can connect with and learn from the real you.

It's important to note that many young people also learn from and find support within their peer groups. This is a natural part of growing up and carving out their identity. However, it's also something we should encourage them to consider carefully. Most teens don't yet understand the *power of proximity,* or the idea that who we spend time around is who we end up emulating. This means if youth connect with someone with wisdom, experience, and shared values, they exponentially increase the likelihood of their success. Conversely, if a young person spends their time around peers with no clear goals, who don't share their values and are consistently getting into trouble, they are likely to be dragged down too.

> "Most teens don't understand that who we spend our time around is who we end up emulating."

Energy and attitude are contagious. Therefore, we should impart positive, constructive, and supportive energy to our youth. Additionally, we should model surrounding ourselves with people who can aid us in reaching our goals, and help our youth do the same.

Mentor Reflections:

1. When have you called on a lifeline in your life? Who supported you at that moment? Share your story/experience with the youth you work with.
2. What do you have to offer the youth you work with? What skills, experiences, characteristics, and knowledge help you be the best mentor you can be?

Youth Action Steps:

1. Write down the names and contact information (phone number, email, social handles) of 3-5 people who positively impact your life. (If you don't have contact information, ask someone who might be able to connect you to them.)
2. Reach out to these potential mentors. Get to know them, their story, and the wisdom, insight, and encouragement they have to offer. Don't be afraid to let them know you are looking for a mentor to learn and receive support from.

Step 10: Practice Gratitude

"We often take for granted the very things that most deserve our gratitude." – Cynthia Ozick

Gratitude is difficult for many people to understand, especially if they're in a bad headspace or are struggling through hard times. In fact, it can be challenging for many of us to think of things to be grateful for. But I've learned that most of the successful people I know, consistently demonstrate an attitude of graciousness and gratitude.

Whether we have a million dollars or one, gratefulness is something all of us should have. If nothing else, we can be  thankful for our time on this earth, the natural gifts we've been given, or the people in our lives.

I didn't think about gratitude until one of my many international trips. While in Turkey, we practiced in a different location than normal, which wasn't unusual. However, I'd never been in this particular neighborhood before. After the practice, a teammate and I walked back to where we were staying.

On the way, I saw kids playing soccer on a field no larger than someone's average backyard. All around were tires, garbage, and filth, and just beyond the yard was a shanty/tent city that was beginning to pop up in the neighborhood. It was amazing to see the joy and energy not only of these kids but of the whole community. Even as someone from the public housing and projects of New York City, I was awestruck by the level of poverty and hardship I saw. Still, I was even more shocked by the unity and culture of the families and communities I interacted with.

"Gratitude changes how our brains work, impacts how we treat others, and improves our approach to the world and its challenges."

This experience is an ever-present reminder of gratitude. Injustices and inequality are indeed very real, and at the same time, each of us can and should be grateful for what we do have. As mentors and youth leaders, it is our job to help young people practice gratitude. We should be helping them identify things to be grateful for and teaching them that gratitude is, first and foremost, for ourselves. It changes how our brains work, impacts how we treat others, and improves our approach to the world and its challenges. Additionally, it aids in our success and growth, shifting our mindsets and opening us up to receive more abundance, opportunities, and success. Even when life is complicated and seemingly insurmountable challenges arise, a sense of gratitude is an essential skill that will help youth ease the pains of life.

Mentor Reflections:

1. How have you seen gratitude transform your mindset and make a difference in your life?
2. What do you do when you lose sight of your gratitude? How do you practice gratitude when things aren't going your way? Share your practices and tools with the youth you work with.

Youth Action Steps:

1. Set a timer for four minutes and make a list of everything you are grateful for, big or small. What is it like thinking this way?
2. We are often most grateful for the people in our lives. Who do you think is grateful for you? Why?

Conclusion

I hope this book has provided you with thought-provoking questions and concrete action steps to help guide your work with youth. As the stories I have shared demonstrate, basketball was and still is a special part of my life. The lessons learned from the people and places I've encountered have been invaluable to my development as a person. My hope is to pay it forward by continuing to pour into all the youth I can. Still, basketball is my story, and everyone has their own to create and share. The sport was the medium that helped shape me and allowed me to evolve into who I am today. I hope that you are on your own journey of transformation and that you share the lessons you learn with others.

This book in itself is the product of a goal pursued and accomplished. Through the process of writing, I have grown and learned things about myself and my own resilience. Putting my thoughts to paper is more challenging than I thought it would be, but through perseverance, supportive people, and educational resources, I got it done. Who would have ever imagined this former athlete from Far Rockaway Queens would ever write a book? But isn't that the point of it all, helping people find strengths they never thought they possessed?

Mentorship is about using wisdom and experience to guide others along their path and advocating for those we lead. I hope this book aids you in outlining what path is right for you and your mentees and leaves you both feeling more empowered. Overall, I hope our youth mindfully choose and plan their futures and surround themselves with the people, influences, and resources that will help them on their way. If we do our jobs well, they will know they are worthy and powerful. They will understand that success waits for no one and is not owed to anyone but that it can be theirs if they know who they want to be and put in the work. So let's support them in that endeavor and watch them grow, thrive, and succeed.

Acknowledgments

This book would not be possible without the countless people who have helped me tap into my own personal greatness. Though there isn't enough space to thank each of you individually, please know I am forever grateful for your guidance and support.

To my editor and project manager, Chelsea Jackson, thank you for your help in bringing this book to fruition.

To my brother and sister, thank you for your everlasting support and encouragement. Words cannot express how much I appreciate you both. And to my brother "Dolly," your light still shines down on me to this very day.

To my daughters, my life's goal is to empower you to become the best version of yourselves and introduce you to the world you are destined to change!

To Coaches Amir, Webber-Bey, and Weiss, the examples and lessons you imparted were invaluable in my development as a player and a person. I appreciate you.

And finally, a special thanks to my Team Crate brothers, let's continue to change our community. From the Rock, For the Rock!

About the Author

Former professional basketball player Abiodun Rashaun Banjo, M.S. E.D., is an international speaker, entrepreneur, and youth leadership specialist. He has dedicated his life to the betterment of young people locally and globally through mentoring, speaking engagements, and his work in the education and nonprofit sectors, including his current work with Queens-based nonprofit Far Rock Strong. Abiodun has a bachelor's in Business from Quinnipiac University and a master's in School Leadership from Adelphi University. He resides in New York with his wife and two daughters.

To inquire about speaking engagements, consultations, and other requests, please contact Rashaun at
rashaun@prolificconsultingservices.com.

Made in the USA
Columbia, SC
05 September 2024